PACIFIC COAST HORNS

Take Five

TUBA

MUSIC MINUS ONE

4707

SUGGESTIONS FOR USING THIS MMO EDITION

WE HAVE TRIED to create a product that will provide you an easy way to learn and perform these compositions with a full ensemble in the comfort of your own home. The following MMO features and techniques will help you maximize the effectiveness of the MMO practice and performance system:

Because it involves a fixed accompaniment performance, there is an inherent lack of flexibility in tempo. We have observed generally accepted tempi, and always in the originally intended key, but some may wish to perform at a different tempo, or to slow down or speed up the accompaniment for practice purposes; or to alter the piece to a more comfortable key. For maximum flexibility, you can purchase from MMO specialized CD players & recorders which allow variable speed while maintaining proper pitch, and vice versa. This is an indispensable tool for the serious musician and you may wish to look into purchasing this useful piece of equipment for full enjoyment of all your MMO editions.

We want to provide you with the most useful practice and performance accompaniments possible. If you have any suggestions for improving the MMO system, please feel free to contact us. You can reach us by e-mail at *info@musicminusone.com*.

4707

CONTENTS

DISC A COMPLETE VERSION TRACK	DISC A MINUS VERSION TRACK	DISC B -12% SLOW MINUS TRACK	DISC B -25% SLOW MINUS TRACK		PAGE
	14	❶		*Tuning*	
1	15	❷	⑮	*Bugler's Holiday*	4
2	16	❸	⑯	*Barber of Seville Overture*	6
3	17	❹	⑰	*In the Dark*	8
				Big Band Montage II:	
4	18	❺	⑱	*Woodchopper's Ball*	9
5	19	❻	⑲	*Cherry Pink and Apple Blossom White*	9
6	20	❼	⑳	*Begin the Beguine*	10
7	21	❽	㉑	*Opus One*	11
8	22	❾	㉒	*Dream*	12
9	23	❿	㉓	*I Wanna Be Like You*	13
10	24	⓫	㉔	*Operatic Rag*	14
11	25	⓬	㉕	*Take Five*	16
12	26	⓭	㉖	*Flower Duet from 'Lakme''*	17
13	27	⓮	㉗	*When the Saints Go Marching In*	18

©2009 MMO Music Group, Inc. All rights reserved.
ISBN 1-59615-791-7

Tuba

Bugler's Holiday

LEROY ANDERSON
arr. by P. CHAUVIN

©1954 Renewed EMI MILLS MUSIC, INC.
Worldwide Print Rights Administered by ALFRED PUBLISHING CO., INC.
All Rights Reserved. Used by Permission.

The Barber of Seville Overture

Tuba

Gioacchino Rossini
Arr. by Charles Warren

Copyright © 2006 Cimarron Music Press. All rights reserved.
www.cimarronmusic.com Used by permission.

In the Dark

Tuba

Bix Beiderbecke
Arr. by Charles Warren

©1930 (Renewed) EMI ROBBINS CATALOG INC.
All Rights Controlled and Administered by EMI ROBBINS CATALOG INC. (Publishing) and ALFRED PUBLISHING CO., INC. (Print)
All Rights Reserved. Used by Permission.

Big Band Montage II

Woodchopper's Ball, Cherry Pink and Appleblossom White,
Begin the Beguine, Opus One, Dream

Tuba

arr. by P. CHAUVIN

Woodchopper's Ball
By Joe Bishop and Woody Herman
Copyright ©1939, 1943, 1958 UNIVERSAL MUSIC CORP. and H&H MUSIC PUBLISHING
Copyright Renewed
This arrangement Copyright ©2009 UNIVERSAL MUSIC CORP. and H&H MUSIC PUBLISHING
All Rights for H&H MUSIC PUBLISHING Controlled and Administered by PRINCESS MUSIC PUBLISHING CORP.
All Rights Reserved. Used by Permission.

Cherry Pink & Apple Blossom White
French Lyric by JACQUES LARUE English Lyric by Mack David Music by LOUIGUY
©1951 (Renewed) CHAPPELL & CO., INC. and UNIVERSAL POLYGRAM INTERNATIONAL, INC.
All Rights Reserved. Used by Permission.

Begin The Beguine (from "Jubilee")
Words and Music by COLE PORTER
©1935 (Renewed) WB MUSIC CORP.
All Rights Reserved. Used by Permission.

Opus One
written by Sy Oliver
Copyright ©1943 (Renewed) by Embassy Music Corporation (BMI)
International Copyright Secured. All Rights Reserved. Reprinted by Permission.

V. S.

MMO 4707

Dream
Words and Music by JOHNNY MERCER
©1945 (Renewed) THE JOHNNY MERCER FOUNDATION
All Rights Administered by WB MUSIC CORP. (Publishing) and
ALFRED PUBLISHING CO., INC. (Print)
All Rights Reserved. Used by Permission.

I Wanna Be Like You

Words and Music by
Richard M. Sherman and Robert B. Sherman

Tuba

©1963 Wonderland Music Company, Inc.
All Rights Reserved. Used by Permission.

Operatic Rag

Tuba

2 taps - 1 measure   ↓A⏢10⏢24 B⏢11⏢24

Julius Lenzberg - Charles Warren

©2004 Chas Music. All rights reserved.
www.chasmusic.com Used by permission, Music Minus One

Take Five

Tuba

Paul Desmond
arr. by P. CHAUVIN

©1960 (Renewed) Desmond Music Company (USA) and Derry Music Company (Canada)
International Copyright Secured. All Rights Reserved. Used by Permission.

Flower Duet

From "Lakme"

Tuba

Leo Delibes
Arr. by Charles Warren

Copyright © 2007 Cimarron Music Press. All rights reserved.
www.cimarronmusic.com Used by permission.

When the Saints Go Marching In

18

Tuba

Traditional

©2007 Pacific Coast Horns. All rights reserved. Used by permission.

MMO 4707

MUSIC MINUS ONE

50 Executive Boulevard
Elmsford, New York 10523-1325
1.800.669.7464 (U.S.)/914.592.1188 (International)

www.musicminusone.com
e-mail: mmogroup@musicminusone.com